TAKI_NG the
BOY SCOUTS
to WAR

TAKING the BOY SCOUTS to WAR

The Short Tale of a Long Journey to Afghanistan

Oritse Justin Uku

Foreword by Christopher Garvin

OFFICIUM PUBLISHING
CHICAGO

ISBN: 1-942188-00-5
ISBN-13: 978-1-942188-00-1
Library of Congress Control Number: 2014918723
LCCN Imprint Name: Chicago, Illinois

To my mother, Celeste-Linguere,
who sent both of her children to war,

and

my brother, Gboyega,
who was the first of us to deploy.

CONTENT

FOREWORD

I met Oritse Uku in the summer of 2008. We both had been recalled by the US Army and assigned to Fort Riley, Kansas, in order to complete a combat advisor's course and prepare for a deployment to Afghanistan. I had been assigned a room in the barracks, and Uku happened to be my roommate and battle buddy. I could have not asked for a better person to be paired with.

After only a few minutes of speaking with him, I knew he was a competent and intelligent man, which he later demonstrated in Afghanistan. Oritse carried himself like a textbook military officer, and you could tell he was a man of integrity. While conducting our predeployment training, we were inseparable, to the point that one of our senior officers referred to us as "hetero life partners."

We completed our training together and deployed, where we were then sent our separate ways. Uku, being a detail-orientated and result-producing military intelligence officer, was assigned as the ARSIC-West intelligence officer and I was sent to Farah, Afghanistan to serve as the leader of an Embedded Training Team.

We went months without seeing each other, until one day I got word that he was being sent down to be part of my team for a few months. My team and I were so excited to have him join us that we fought through a Taliban stronghold just to get him.

Immediately after he joined our team, we found ourselves in one of the largest firefights I have ever been in, and the fights continued until the day he left to go home. Uku and I have been through a lot together, be it firefights or living on a forward operating base with no air conditioning in 130-degree heat.

Through everything, I am privileged to have served with such a fine man and officer. Uku, to this day, is one of the best men I know, and I am honored to call him my friend.

Christopher Garvin
Leesburg, Virginia
August 25, 2014

PREFACE

My former commander, Colonel John Bessler, was the first person I heard liken mentoring the Afghan National Security Forces (ANSF) to "taking the boy scouts to war." I don't know if he coined the term, but the expression was sadly appropriate. Counter-insurgency is considered to be the graduate degree level of warfare. It's not nearly as simple as traditional force-on-force conflict. Yet we are trying to prepare this underequipped, undertrained, underpaid and undereducated security force to fight graduate-level battles, when they are still struggling to get the basics down.

Afghanistan is not Iraq. It was not a functioning country before we got there. There are some relatively cosmopolitan cities like Kabul, Herat and Mazar-i-Sharif. However, there are a lot of villages that would make you think you were in the 14th century if not for the automobiles, cell phones and AK-47s. I personally believe that America is going to be in Afghanistan for a long time to come.

The Afghans are trying to build a functioning government from scratch. There are problems and corruption. There are also a lot of good people who want to make their country a better place. They will fail without the help of the United States. The goal is to convince the people of Afghanistan that their government can protect them and provide for them. Sometimes, the presence of a small number of American mentors makes the difference for the ANSF between victory and defeat in combat against the Taliban.

I imagine that every American remembers where he or she was on Sept. 11th, 2001. I was in the middle of our capstone field training exercise in Basic Combat Training at Fort Knox, Kentucky. On Sept. 14th, 2001, I was on a plane to Officer Candidate School (OCS) in my dress green uniform. Like many young warriors today, nearly the entirety of my service has been in a wartime Army.

Opponents of the war in Afghanistan often call it "another Vietnam". While there are some striking similarities, this view is overly simplistic and fails to look beyond the superficial characteristics of the two conflicts. When I speak to Vietnam veterans, I'm amazed by the similarities of dealing with the South Vietnamese Army and the Afghan National Army. However, Afghanistan is not a proxy war rooted in the Cold War and post-colonial conflict.

Average Afghans have no interest in international politics or policy. They simply want to be able to raise their families in peace and have enough money to support those families and enough food to feed them. Most importantly, they want to be free from violence, extortion and fear.

Col. Bessler asked me before I redeployed if I was going to write a book. I was rather surprised by the question and had no plan to do so at the time. It was my friends at the National Speakers Association who convinced me that I should do so. People like Dale Collie, Mark Eaton and Steve Tyra convinced me to tell my story.

Personally, I think my story is fairly typical. I was recalled to the Army and served in direct combat with the Taliban. As I begin this account, it has been exactly 60 days since the last time anyone has shot at me with an AK-47, a rocket propelled grenade or a mortar. It's not like the movies. In the words of Sergeant Nolan T. Anderson, "Combat ain't cool. It's exciting, but it ain't cool."

This is a story the American public is not familiar with. I have not met anyone who was even aware that the military could recall service members, with the exception of other veterans. I've been fortunate to serve with some brave warriors. It takes a special breed to move towards the sound of gunfire, when everyone else is running away.

Oritse Justin Uku

August 10, 2009

ACKNOWLEDGMENTS

Thank you to everyone who helped bring this book to fruition. It would not have been possible without the encouragement and guidance of Dale Collie and my mother, Celeste-Linguere.

Editing by Logan T. Johnston III. Cover design by Aaryn Goldbaum. Back cover photo by Michael Schacht. Additional thanks to Terry Brock and Michael Sands.

TAKING the BOY SCOUTS to WAR

1 THE LETTER

It was January 13, 2008 when I received the letter. This was the letter that every former soldier dreads. It had been sixteen months since I'd left the army to attend graduate school. Most of the junior officers I knew were doing the same thing. Many of us were headed to business school or law school, but we were all trying to move on with life after the army.

On this particular night, I'd just flown back to Boston after spending the holidays with my family in Phoenix. I'd always been stationed overseas, so this was only the second holiday season I'd spent with my family in the previous six years. To celebrate my return to Boston and the beginning of my final semester of business school, I went out for drinks that night with my classmate and good friend, Patrick Long. We hung out until after 1:00 a.m., said our good-nights, and each went home. When I climbed into bed at 2:00 a.m., I was in a good mood. Then I saw it.

Lying on the floor next to my bed was a FedEx envelope. My roommate, Stacey, had put it there for me while I was home for the holidays. As I picked up the envelope, a sense of absolute panic overtook me. It was from the Department of the Army, addressed to Captain Oritse J. Uku. I'd received plenty of mail from the army since I'd gotten out in September 2006, usually from Army National Guard or Army Reserve units seeking to recruit young officers fresh off active duty. There was a shortage of military intelligence officers like me, so that was to be expected. This was different, though.

After you get out, you hear about the FedEx envelope. When the army is recalling you back to active duty, using Federal Express rather than the US Postal Service seems to come in handy. It's never welcome news, so by using FedEx, someone has to sign for the envelope, and you can't claim you didn't receive your orders.

It was 2:00 a.m. and there was nothing I could do about the situation, so I figured I'd go to sleep and open the envelope in the morning. I proceeded to lay there for the next sixty minutes, completely unable to sleep. I gave up trying and got up to face the inevitable bad news. I pulled that little red string across the top of the envelope hoping for the best, but fully expecting the worst. I got the worst.

Not many people outside of the military are familiar with the Individual Ready Reserve (IRR) program. It is a program that allows the military to recall service members after they've left the service, during times of war. All branches of the military have an IRR program, but as far as I know, only the army and the marines have been recalling their service members due to the Global War on Terror.

Understandably, no one appears to want a military draft. The United States has worked hard to create a professional military in the post-Vietnam era. For politicians, it seems like political suicide to suggest a draft. I've never met a military leader who liked the idea. And I'm certain that all those military age males who aren't even keeping track of what's going on in Iraq and

Afghanistan have no interest in a draft. So how do you deal with manning shortages in a two-front war with no draft? You recall IRR soldiers and marines. It's not a draft, because they are still under commitment, and it doesn't seem to draw any media attention whatsoever.

So now I was another casualty of the IRR program. In fact, I and the others like me would be known as IRR soldiers and IRR officers. That status would differentiate us from the active duty, National Guard, and reserves. We were there to do our duty, but we were not volunteers.

As I caught my breath and better examined the orders that had just turned my world upside down, I noticed that they were dated three weeks prior. I was supposed to report for duty at Fort Jackson, South Carolina in six days! I had four months until I was going to graduate with my MBA. I had an apartment with a roommate. My family lived on the other side of the country. Yet I was supposed to uproot and report, to go God knows where, in six days! My night had gone from pretty good to terribly bad in a little over an hour. I was now an IRR officer. Back in the service.

2 READY RESERVE

May 6, 2005 was the beginning of the end of my career as an active duty army officer. I was serving as the battalion intelligence officer for 2d Military Intelligence Battalion in Darmstadt, Germany. I was a first lieutenant at the time, and that afternoon, my battalion had just returned from a field training exercise. I went up to my office with eager anticipation, as I was expecting to receive two important e-mails. As luck would have it, they had both arrived.

I opened the first e-mail and was greeted with good news. I would be promoted to the rank of captain the following month. Making captain in thirty-nine months was faster than officers were promoted during the Cold War, but the junior officers knew there was currently a lot of attrition in that rank. If you can't retain captains, you can at least make captains faster.

A feeling of nervous excitement passed over me as I opened the second e-mail. My officer year group was finally eligible to apply for selection to become Special Forces officers. I'd been waiting three years for this moment. I figured that I'd be able to bring a different perspective to a Special Forces assignment as an intelligence officer. I believed most intelligence officers weren't interested in that sort of thing, so it would help to differentiate me. I read the list from top to bottom. Then I read it again. I was not on it. I'd been waiting three years for this moment, and I wasn't even going to get a chance to try out.

The question before me was "Now what?" My army career seemed to be hallmarked by volunteering for everything, but not getting to do any of it. I'd volunteered for a peacetime army, but graduated from basic combat training on September 14, 2001. Thus, I'd served in a wartime army ever since. At Officer Candidate School in 2001, I requested to be assigned to the 82nd Airborne Division or 101st Airborne Division. Those units would be involved with the fight in Afghanistan. I, however, would be going to South Korea. Between 2002 and 2003, I tried to get an assignment at the 75th Ranger Regiment. It would have been a great assignment, as a battalion assistant intelligence officer, but when it was time to get my orders for Ranger School, no one would return my e-mails. I found out a couple of years later that my point of contact had deployed, and clearly had no out of office reply set.

In 2004, I'd volunteered for a task force that was deploying to Afghanistan, but I wasn't taken. In early 2005, I thought my unit would be going to Iraq, but that didn't happen. Now, I'd volunteered to become a Special Forces officer and wasn't getting a chance to do that.

I spoke to my leadership. The commander, executive officer, and operations officer were the only other people in the headquarters, as everyone else had been released for the day. They tried to cheer me up and presented some other opportunities, but it all seemed like dangling the proverbial carrot just a bit further ahead of me. I'd be eligible for this program or that job in a couple of years. I was a frustrated twenty-five-year-old officer. I had watched the invasion of Iraq on CNN from South Korea in 2003, and for some reason never got to deploy or get into the fight when everyone around me was.

When conducting my intelligence training at Fort Huachuca, Arizona as a newly minted second lieutenant in 2002, I read *Special Forces: A Guided Tour of US Army Special Forces* by Tom Clancy and John Gresham. At the time, I thought it was odd that they claimed most soldiers who don't get selected for Special Forces subsequently leave the army. But that's ultimately what I did.

I went back and forth debating options for my future, and had been promoted to captain by the time I decided to leave active duty and go to graduate school. Most of my officer friends in Germany were already on an outbound trajectory. My best friends consisted of a small group, including Captains Luis Rodriguez, Joseph Sarto, Jonté Harrell, and Jeff Lau. Luis and Joe had already left the army and headed back to the States. Jonté and Jeff were both planning to depart the army a year after me, though Jonté was on the hook for a second Iraq rotation before then.

I decided to keep my plans to myself for as long as possible. I'd seen enough people leave the army to know there were some career army personnel who could make your life more difficult. First, there are some people who think the army has a monopoly on good people. Once you're no longer in the army, they think you're no longer a good person. Second, there are people who will make it their job to try to talk you out of your decision until the day you leave.

Of course, there are also those who will opt not to do you any professional favors or give you any favorable actions because you're getting out, anyway. Not everyone is like that, but there are enough of them out there that you want to avoid having to deal with them. Like any good intelligence officer, I chose to err on the side of secrecy.

All active duty soldiers are familiar with the Individual Ready Reserve. It's a mandatory part of our military contract, though my understanding of it at the time didn't quite match up with the reality. I signed a delayed entry contract in June 2000, prior to my senior year of college, meaning that even though I'd signed my contract to enlist for Officer Candidate School (OCS), I wouldn't report for training until I'd graduated college.

The way my recruiter explained it to me was that I could be recalled up to eight years after I'd entered the army. So, if I served six years of active duty, I could be recalled for two years after that. It seemed pretty moot at the time. We were at peace, and didn't foresee any wars on the horizon. The recruiter also mentioned a couple of things that weren't quite true. He said that it would take something like World War III for the President to initiate an IRR recall.

In hindsight, that was obviously an exaggeration, but it's probably inappropriate for a recruiter to state the criteria for the President to make most any military decision. This staff sergeant also stated that the last time an IRR recall was enacted was during the Vietnam War. Also untrue. There was an IRR recall as recently as Desert Storm. But when you don't expect to see a full-blown war anytime soon, the criteria for an IRR recall is the least of your worries.

By the time my friends and I were planning to leave the army in 2005, we were aware that the IRR program was alive and well. There was a massive IRR recall in support of Operation Iraqi Freedom (OIF). There was a surprise, though. A bunch of officers got recalled on a technicality. Though their eight-year commitment was up, those officers hadn't resigned their commissions, so they were still eligible to be recalled. I have yet to meet an army officer who had ever heard about this technicality prior to the recall of these very surprised individuals. Those of us on active duty, however, took note: once your eight years are up, make sure to formally resign your commission.

That still left you with the decision of what to do prior to the end of your eight-year commitment. I would be leaving active duty with nearly five-and-a-half years of service. Does one join the National Guard or the Army Reserves? They didn't have the best reputations with active duty personnel. Besides, this wasn't the Vietnam War, where signing up for the Guard would keep you out of the war. The Guard and Reserves were deploying and fighting alongside their active duty brethren.

The Reserve Component Recruiter I met with in Germany told me of a program where I could sign up with a reserve component unit and decrease my remaining IRR time by one year. I would also be nondeployable for the first two years. I wasn't all that eager to be in the Guard or Reserves while I was in school, but virtually guaranteeing that I would not get recalled seemed like too good an opportunity to pass up.

Unfortunately, he incorrectly told me that I was ineligible for the program when I went back to sign up. So with some bad information in my back pocket, I decided to roll the dice and just enter the IRR pool, hoping for the best.

3 BACK IN UNIFORM

I reported for duty at Fort Jackson, South Carolina on the warm, muggy Sunday afternoon of July 20, 2008. Six months prior, the week following the receipt of my recall orders had been unimaginably stressful and emotional. I petitioned to the offices of Senator John McCain of Arizona, my home state, and Senator Edward Kennedy of Massachusetts. I told their staffs that I was not trying to get out of this recall and subsequent deployment, I just wanted to graduate from business school first. I only had four months left, and I would report for duty the day after graduation if the army wanted me to. Deans Jeff Ringuest and Warren Zola at the Carroll Graduate School of Management did their best to help interface with

Senator Kennedy's office, but nobody seemed to be able to get a delay from the army for me in the few days that I had available.

Friday, January 18th was the last business day prior to my report date that Sunday, and all seemed hopeless. That afternoon, I went back to my apartment to pack my duffel bags. I'd been storing my army uniforms and equipment since I'd gotten out. It looked like, despite my hopes, I was going to be using them again in a couple of days. My last ditch effort that overcast Friday afternoon was to call the US Army Human Resources Command (HRC). I figured it was a long shot, but I'd tried everything else. As fate would have it, I reached a sergeant first class who helped me get a stay of execution.

When I eventually reported for duty that muggy Sunday afternoon in South Carolina, I was relatively content. I had a newly earned MBA behind me, and had enough time to vacation in Australia. All in all, I considered myself to be pretty lucky.

I knew I was deploying to Afghanistan, and was actually a bit relieved about it. It's not that I was going to Afghanistan rather than Iraq. It was that I was going at all. Almost all of my active duty service had been during a time of war, yet I was never deployed. I served in South Korea and Germany, but never in a combat zone. So when I got out, everyone who ever heard that I was in the army automatically asked, "Were you in Iraq?" It was an awkward question to answer all the time. It felt like trying to tell people I wasn't a coward who'd been avoiding the war, I was just an officer who seemed to repeatedly be in units that didn't deploy me.

I've met veterans who served in Germany during the Vietnam War. They give that same sort of almost apologetic explanation. I had expected to have to deal with that for the rest of my life. You see this little bit of disappointment in people's eyes when they realize they didn't just meet a combat veteran. But I wouldn't have to deal with that any more. After this deployment, I could simply answer the question, "Were you in Iraq?" with the answer, "No, I was in Afghanistan." I'd be able to hold my head a little higher afterward.

Between officers I knew and those who were one degree of separation away, I knew of about a dozen captains who'd been recalled in the first half of 2008. Therefore, I expected to be at Fort Jackson with a bunch of other captains. That, however, was not the case. In fact, I was the only captain in my group. All the other officers were retirees. Majors, lieutenant colonels, colonels—in fact, there was one warrant officer who'd fought in Vietnam who was trying to get a medical waiver to deploy. I knew that young soldiers and officers were being recalled, but I had no idea that retirees were being recalled *en masse* as well.

The recall medical evaluation generally consists of younger people playing up their physical ailments so they don't have to deploy, and older people playing down their ailments for the exact opposite reason. Since I wasn't trying to get out of anything, the process was pretty simple for me. I wasn't a volunteer, but I wasn't a draftee, either. I was a professional officer who knew about the IRR clause in his contract, just like everybody else. The funny thing is that when I got out, it took me three months to get used to being a civilian. After being recalled, it only took two weeks to get used to being an army officer again.

Besides boredom, what I'll always remember about being at Fort Jackson was watching the US Navy personnel being trained for ground missions in Iraq and Afghanistan. They basically put all these sailors and navy officers through basic training. It was funny to watch, because they were so out of their element. I'm sure they're adept at navy tasks, but army operations seemed totally foreign to them. I'll fully admit that if I were put on a navy ship, I wouldn't have a clue what I was doing. As it is, it doesn't look like that will ever happen. The rivalry between services is like a sibling rivalry. You wish them the best, but still make fun of them every chance you get. I quietly smiled to myself one day when I overheard one sailor tell another that she had a newfound respect for the army.

4 TRANSITION TEAMS

When I started training at Fort Riley, Kansas on August 25, 2008, I had been on a whirlwind tour of military posts. I'd been sent to three different army bases in three different states over the course of six weeks. Since I'm a military intelligence officer, I was sent to the Intelligence School at Fort Huachuca, Arizona for refresher training. The entire concept baffled me. I'd been out of the army for a mere twenty-two months. Did they think I'd forgotten how to do my job?

Moreover, no one at the schoolhouse had any clue what refresher training was supposed to mean. Despite their best efforts, they couldn't get hold of anyone who could tell them what it was, either. In proof that the army really is a small world, I ran into CW3 Alan Morano, who was at 2d Military Intelligence Battalion in Germany with me. He always struck me as a good guy, and now he was an instructor at the schoolhouse. When Al told me that he would take care of me, I was comforted.

They threw me into the Military Intelligence Captain's Career Course, which for the most part simply covered the same material I'd been taught six-and-a-half years earlier, as a second lieutenant. Relevant, if I was planning on fighting a Soviet tank brigade. Not so relevant to anything I would likely encounter in Afghanistan.

However, the three weeks spent at Fort Huachuca was not a complete waste, for two reasons. First, I'm from Phoenix, Arizona, which is a quick three-hour drive away, so I was able to visit my mother, stepfather, and brother (an OIF veteran) every weekend. That's the sort of thing you really appreciate immediately prior to deployment. Second, Al got me placed into a week-long class about transition teams.

I refer to transition teams as the exit strategy for both Iraq and Afghanistan. They are called Military Transition Teams (MiTTs) for Iraq. In Afghanistan, Embedded Transition Teams (ETTs) work with the Afghan National

Army (ANA), and Police Mentor Teams (PMTs) work with the Afghan National Police (ANP). Despite all the different acronyms, they all have the same basic mission: mentor host nation forces, so that they are able to function self-sufficiently and allow the withdrawal of allied forces.

I was being assigned to an ETT headed to Afghanistan, so this would be particularly relevant training. In fact, despite the months that I would spend training at Fort Riley, this informal class, taught by other MICCC students who had previously deployed on transition teams, was the best bit of predeployment training I would receive. It caught my attention that dealing with Afghan forces was a bit like dealing with the Boy Scouts. Sometimes you'd have to hold their hands to get them through a challenge. Often, they would turn to their mentors for support, rather than dealing with the challenges of their own support military. Then, of course, there was the matter of what I call "good ol' Afghan betrayal."

Officers who had been on transition teams in Afghanistan repeatedly warned to never completely disarm around your mentored forces, especially the

Afghan National Police. All it takes is for one official to make a deal with the Taliban and you could end up dead. Transition team members would be assigned an M4 assault rifle and an M9 Berretta .9 mm pistol. It was recommended to at least keep that loaded pistol with you at all times while in host nation facilities. That was a lesson that stuck with me. I had no intention of being the guy who let his guard down and got killed in a meeting.

5 MEETING THE TEAM

America was not at war. The American military was at war, but the country as a whole was not. That was my personal sentiment, but every soldier I ever mentioned it to seemed to agree. How else could you explain why American warriors were asked to sacrifice so much, but American civilians so little? During World War II, the entire country was mobilized for war. Twelve percent of the country was in uniform (versus less than 0.5 percent today). But more to the point, the war actually affected people's everyday lives at home. It shocked me when I first left the service how little the wars in Afghanistan and Iraq affected anyone at home (besides military families).

Like most junior officers, I was not old enough to remember World War II, the Korean War, the Vietnam War, Grenada, or even Panama. I was old enough to remember the Gulf War, though; to remember how it captivated our attention, and how we'd watch the news every night to find out the latest and greatest. That was a short war, though. Perhaps it was too much to expect people to still care after seven years of war. That is the question I would come to hear soldiers discuss time and time again while training and deployed. Do Americans even care anymore?

I finally started my ETT training at Fort Riley on August 25, 2008. It was my first interaction with other officers in my situation. Though my twenty-man ETT was being filled by the Illinois National Guard, four of the six captains on the team were IRR. Illinois was manning a number of ETTs and PMTs, but supposedly could not fill all the positions. That's where the IRRs came in. As one would expect, we quickly began to trade stories as to how we got there.

Captain Chris Garvin, an Oklahoma native, had actually been stationed at Fort Riley before. We had served in Korea at about the same time, and at Fort Riley.

During the 2003 invasion of Iraq, he led a platoon from 1st Brigade, 1st Infantry Division's Brigade Reconnaissance Troop. He was an armor officer through and through, but had led a lot of combat missions from inside a HMMWV. Chris and I would later fight together in what the Associated Press would call a "fierce ground battle" in Farah province.

Captain Eric Vinitsky, from Dorchester, Massachusetts, was another Iraq veteran. In college and business school, I'd spent a combined five years in Boston (though I studied abroad one year in Australia), and I've never heard a Boston accent that heavy. Several times, I'd have to translate for the rest of the team when they couldn't understand what he was saying. Eric was a graduate of the US Merchant Marine Academy, and had actually served as a merchant marine prior to joining the army. Eric would eventually be involved in fighting so close in Badghis province that he would actually throw hand grenades at the enemy.

Captain Jacob Bennington was the nicest guy you could ever met. Honestly, I occasionally wondered if he was too nice to be an army officer. Like me, Jake had managed to go his entire active duty time without deploying, more by chance than design. Since leaving the army, both he and his wife were studying to be teachers.

The one thing we all had in common is that we'd moved on with our lives. Chris was the manager for a Kmart in Glendive, Montana. (I was surprised to find out this paid a lot more than the army.) Eric was a firefighter and an emergency medical technician (EMT) for the Boston Fire Department. Jake was teaching in Colorado Springs, CO. We'd all been violently yanked out of our lives by our IRR recalls. The funny thing is that it's like when Kennedy was assassinated, or when O.J. was acquitted. Everybody remembers vividly exactly where he was and what he was doing when the recall letter came.

I was truly impressed that everyone was very professional about the experience. Sure, no one was especially excited to be there, but people weren't whining. They weren't dragging their heels. They weren't trying to get out of anything. We were all there to do our duty and go home.

6 THE COUNT

My team at Fort Riley was commanded by Lieutenant Colonel Henry "Buck" Dixon. Lt. Col. Dixon forced me to rethink the bad things that I'd heard about the National Guard. He was an even-keeled, intelligent, fun leader. He was an Iraq veteran, a battalion commander back in Illinois, and a country lawyer in his civilian life. He ended up being one of the best officers I'd ever worked for.

Lt. Col. Dixon and Sergeant Major Howe had their hands full dealing with this team of officers and noncommissioned officers (i.e., sergeants) who were going through training. This was the normal makeup of a transition team. The upside is that you get a lot of experience and maturity in a small team element. The downside is that when you have a team full of leaders, everyone is used to being in charge. You get a lot of comments that begin with "Well, at my last unit..." or "When I was in Iraq..." or "That's not how I used to do the thing..." It was a little bit like herding cats, but by and large, the team got along well.

Occasionally, team members would embark on insightful debates sparked by Captain Jonathan Harvey. More often, team members would be sucked into debates of utter nonsense, also sparked by John. I had a general rule not to get involved in such debates unless I knew what I was talking about. One afternoon, John was going on about the financial industry, as we had some down time in the barracks. As was my practice, I did my best not to get involved with the debate, though I considered his position to be uninformed. John came over to my bunk to draw me into the debate.

Others considered this an ill-advised move. It was common knowledge that I'd just gotten an MBA specializing in corporate finance, and had interned the previous summer in private banking. However, people did perk up in anticipation of a show. The ensuing onslaught would have made a high school debate team coach proud. It definitely amused my teammates. This is how time was spent at Fort Riley.

We shared a forty-man open bay with another team. All these senior personnel were stacked in there on bunk beds, like basic trainees. By and large, we weren't all that impressed with the training. The last week of it was pretty good, but the rest seemed like a lot of filler.

The two months we spent at Fort Riley did, however, allow us to get to know our teammates on these slightly hodgepodge teams. Even though the teams would ultimately be broken up when we got to Afghanistan, it allowed us to foster friendships that would last beyond the deployment. Major John "Doc" Fulk and I ended up finding plenty in common, as we both tended to consider ourselves connoisseurs of life. Doc was our physician's assistant, and was prone to expensive tastes. The result was a number of discussions that would drive Eric, with his distinctly blue-collar tastes, absolutely crazy.

The mix of personnel did lead to a slight culture clash. All six of our captains, including Steve Olsen (later promoted to major), grew up on active duty. John and Steve joined the Illinois National Guard after leaving active duty. There was often bewilderment as to how the Guard operates. It clearly had some good people, but it had some issues as an organization. One thing that always got Eric riled up was the fact that Illinois had increased the dwell time (the minimum amount of time between deployments) for their soldiers by one year. The theory was that all IRR recalls were because some general in Illinois wanted to give his soldiers extra time between deployments.

At some time during our stay at Riley, the team gave me the nickname Count Uku, apparently based on the *Star Wars* character Count Dooku. The other officers had been calling me Count Uku for some time before I found out, but it was hilarious. My stepbrother was jealous that he didn't have a *Star Wars* based nickname. From then on, officers from my team would simply refer to me as Count. Jake got the nickname Bennington Bear. It seemed to be based on the stuffed animal, rather than the wild one.

On a transition team, since everyone is senior, there obviously aren't any junior soldiers. That means people have to train for tasks they normally would not do, based on their rank. For mounted combat patrols, that meant driving and gunning. For this reason, we all got HMMWV licenses. I've driven in HMMWVs plenty during my career, but I was always the truck commander (in the front passenger seat) rather than the driver. I had soldiers to drive. Some units, such as my first unit, even had rules that officers don't drive. Those rules were usually the result of officers crashing HMMWVs.

Lt. Col. Dixon wanted to make sure that those of us who didn't have much experience driving HMMWVs were the primary drivers as we went through training. That naturally included me, so I would drive a HMMWV on almost all our training missions, while Chris Garvin would command it. The relationship worked out fine, as Chris and I were increasingly good friends. This, however, was a job I grew more and more weary of.

During those predawn morning missions, you had to actually be awake if you were the driver. Everyone was supposed to be awake, but the backseat is much more forgiving of people dozing off. Despite the fact that I would have loved a break from driving, all those hours I spent behind that wheel showed foresight on Lt. Col. Dixon's part. Months later, I would serve as a driver in combat, which is much less forgiving than Fort Riley.

The fact that I needed to learn how to drive a HMMWV foreshadowed things to come. There are plenty of tasks officers normally don't take part in, simply because 1) we have soldiers to do them, and 2) we're busy doing other things, like planning. However, the ETT mission would break down some of those officer/enlisted barriers, and is definitely not for those whose ego is too closely associated with his rank.

Sometimes it would be a captain's job to prepare the truck to go out on a mission. That wouldn't happen at a conventional unit. Sometimes an officer would take direction from enlisted men with more experience in a given subject. Regardless, you'll find a lot more familiarity between officers and NCOs on transition teams than you'll find elsewhere. It just has to do with that small unit dynamic. Instead of having five officers and 200 enlisted men in a company, you might have four officers and eight enlisted men (all NCOs) on a transition team.

An example of the familiarity that would develop was the fact that officers and NCOs who were well acquainted would start to refer to each other by simply their surnames. Staff Sergeant Melson would be just Melson. Captain Garvin would be Garvin. Major Fulk would be Doc. I would just be Uku (only the officers called me Count). Using a nickname is something I never would tolerate in a conventional unit, but it was just part of normal existence in the transition teams. Rank was respected, but often wasn't used.

7 WEST BOUND

During the course of our time at Fort Riley, my team found out we were supposed to go to Herat, a wealthy city in western Afghanistan. Herat was a popular entry point between Iran and Afghanistan. The west of Afghanistan, as far as the International Security Assistance Force (ISAF) was concerned, was Italian and Spanish battlespace. The forces from those countries had operational control of Herat, Farah, Badghis, and Ghor provinces.

On October 2, 2008, I mentioned that I was heading to Herat to my best friend from college, Jonathan Baker. Jon was a former US Army captain who had served in both Iraq and Afghanistan with the 173rd Airborne

Brigade. His response was that "Herat is like the ultimate green zone…that's where the Italians play volleyball." This reference to the green zone safe haven in Iraq pretty well summarized the popular opinion that neither the Taliban nor the Italian army were doing much in Herat province.

Jon's statement also touches on the opinion about many of our ISAF allies held by US service members. If you ask a US service member in Afghanistan what ISAF stands for, you'll hear a good variety of amusing responses: I Suck At Fighting, I Saw Americans Fight, I Stole American Food, I Sunbathe At FOBs, etc.

While the jokes slightly diminish the efforts of our allies, they do point out the frustration with how our allies choose to operate. The jokes don't reflect US sentiment regarding all of our allies in ISAF, but it seems that a number of allied countries believe they are in Afghanistan for peacekeeping. Others believe they are there for fighting. The general feeling is that if you are going to get into a fight, you can depend on the British, the Canadians, the Australians, and the Dutch.

During my team's time at Fort Riley, it was decided that a number of us would be assigned to the staff of

Afghan Regional Security Integration Command (ARSIC)–West, including me. ARSIC–West, commanded by Colonel John Bessler, was the headquarters for all US transition teams in the west. This headquarters assignment was a disappointment to most everyone who had been tagged to stay on staff.

As a result, when we flew out of Kansas City en route to Afghanistan early on the morning of November 13, I was feeling a bit deflated. There was the normal excitement of finally deploying, finally being done with six weeks of training. There was the normal stress on my personal relationships, particularly with my mother and my then fiancée. Also, it occurred to me that I could get killed in Afghanistan, so for the first time I really felt scared. On top of all that, there was a brewing frustration that once again I was going to be put on a staff assignment, away from the action. There were so many people who were interested in avoiding dangerous situations, yet somehow I kept being sheltered away at desk jobs.

Fortune did smile on me a bit as I made the trek to Herat. It only took me three days to get there. We had a layover in Shannon, Ireland, and spent only two days at

Manas Air Base in Kyrgyzstan. I was truly fortunate to spend less than twenty-four hours in Kabul waiting for a flight. Others spent over a week there. One thing that people don't appreciate about deployment, unless they've been there, is the duffel bag drag. It's not like commercial travel. We had four duffel bags, a rucksack, body armor, a Kevlar helmet, and two weapons that we had to drag along with us everywhere until we got to our final destination. One can easily be dragging 300–400 pounds of baggage and equipment around the world for a week, or longer.

8 YELLOWSTONE TWO

My arrival in Herat revealed a landscape completely contrary to what I'd heard about from Afghanistan veterans. Instead of vast, snow-capped mountains and unforgiving altitude, there were wide deserts. Of course, as a guy who grew up in Phoenix, Arizona, I knew that deserts could get very cold. Unfortunately, that didn't give me enough foresight to pack cold-weather gear in my carry-on bag. I was freezing, as the contingent that flew into Herat on November 16 ended up stranded at the airfield for hours. The convoy from Camp Stone that was coming to pick us up had been hit by a suicide vehicle-borne improvised explosive device (SVBIED)—a suicide car bomb. So much for the "ultimate green zone."

Two American soldiers were wounded in that attack. If the suicide bomber had come a little later, I would have been in the convoy on the way back to Camp Stone when he hit it. I learned that ten kilometer stretch of road between Camp Arena and Camp Stone was the mostly heavily SVBIED'd stretch of road in the entire west.

ARSIC–West would be the third S-2 shop (Intelligence Staff Section) that I'd run, but I was still a bit apprehensive, as it was the first time I'd done so in a combat zone. My call sign was Yellowstone Two (the number two signified that I was the ARSIC S-2). Sergeant First Class David Barron was a great mentor in getting me settled into the role. Sergeant Barron was an infantryman, a scout, and a sniper, but he'd been serving as NCO in charge of the S-2 shop for months.

Barron may not have had a formal intel background, but he excelled at human intelligence collection. He was exceedingly proficient at getting information from Afghans, and judging the character of civilians and government officials. In addition, his infantry background gave him a level of aggressiveness that I truly appreciated. While there were plenty of leaders at Camp Stone who believed that as mentors we shouldn't be involved with directly fighting the Taliban, Barron and I agreed that we shouldn't run from the Taliban, either. That can lead the Taliban to believe the Americans are afraid of them. As an American soldier, if I'm better trained, armed, and equipped, why should I run from a guy in flip-flops with an AK-47 who's older than I am?

I might not have volunteered for this particular deployment, but I'm still a professional. If I'm going to be pulled back to serve, then I'm going to do it right. Like General Patton said, "I'm a soldier. I fight where I am told, and I win where I fight."

9 HERAT

The next several months in Herat can be best described as a combination of mistrust, heartbreak, and frustration. As Sergeant Barron and the other men I'd inherited in my S-2 shop rotated back to the States, I rebuilt and trained the new crop of military intelligence personnel, consisting of soldiers, sailors, and airmen, which I'd received for our mission. (In further proof that it is indeed a small army, one of my new NCOs, Sergeant Lloyd, and I realized that I'd actually been his company executive officer as a first lieutenant in Germany.)

It was rather difficult to figure out who to trust. For starters, among the Afghan leaders, there was the disconcerting fact that the senior Afghan National Army,

Herat police, and Taliban commanders seemed to all have personal relationships with each other. I would joke they all went to high school together, but that really wasn't too far off the mark. Most of them had fought together in the Mujahedeen against the Soviets. In fact, I don't think senior Afghan army and police commanders who didn't fight in the Mujahedeen garnered as much respect with their peers.

There were too many instances that just didn't feel right. For example, I ended up dealing with a lot of Afghans I didn't trust at all when we went out on patrol to villages. As the intelligence officer, I would talk to as many locals as I could, collecting information about what was going on in the area and about the Taliban, as well as about local criminals, like the Herat local boogeyman, Gulam Yaya. I had to assume word about me would get back to the Taliban and criminal elements.

Therefore, I opted not to give these random Afghans my real name. Instead, I took an Afghan name. While they could see my captain rank insignia, I removed the name tape from my body armor, and introduced myself as Omar Khan. My concern was that Uku is not a common surname, so I didn't want any ambitious Taliban or other troublemakers to be able to track me down (or worse, a relative of mine) after I redeployed from Afghanistan. Was I being overly cautious? Maybe, but with potential Al-Qaida connections still floating around, and the Islamic Republic of Iran less than a two-hour drive away, caution seemed warranted. Iran was definitely not happy about having the US military in two of its neighbors, and has strong historical and commercial connections with Herat.

I never used the *nom de guerre* Omar Khan in cities or with Afghan officials, so it caught me off guard when the Herat police chief casually mentioned in a meeting that he knew I was Omar Khan. He offered no explanation, just a smile.

Occasionally, while meeting with officials like the police chief, you would have someone snap a picture of you without warning, then disappear back into the crowd in the police headquarters. Not the sort of thing that gives you a warm, fuzzy feeling. Also, we heard frequent stories of American army trainers who were killed by the Afghan soldiers or police they were training. This was the Afghan betrayal I'd heard about. With all this going on, I would never be unarmed in a meeting with any Afghans.

So, on one hand, we had our Afghan partners that we couldn't completely trust, and on the other hand, we had our NATO allies, many of whom didn't seem to take the mission as seriously as the Americans did. The Spanish and Italians had lost people in Afghanistan as well, but they proved to be much more risk averse than the American military.

One humanitarian assistance visit I went on with a team of American soldiers exemplified how heartbreaking and frustrating Afghanistan could be. We knew that Afghan women can live their entire lives without receiving adequate medical attention, especially in the villages. We also knew that the Afghan men didn't want foreign male soldiers talking to their women. We wanted to help, but we knew we had to be culturally sensitive.

For this visit, to a village not too far from the capital of Herat, we had the perfect plan to address all the needs of the villagers. We were bringing clothes and supplies, but the presence of a US Army medical team was the most valuable asset we brought to the village.

Respecting the local traditions, we addressed the village elders with our plan. "We have a team of

American army medical personnel consisting solely of female soldiers. We can set up a tent just off to one side of the village to allow for privacy. We can provide medical care without any of our men seeing your women. May we please provide medical care to your women?"

The answer: no. We would only be permitted to provide medical care to male villagers. I was in utter disbelief. We had done everything to be culturally sensitive, yet they decided their women would receive no help. Their health, which seemed generally poor, was a secondary concern—at best.

It was amazing. In big cities like Herat, you could spot Afghan women in jeans and high heels walking alongside their friends, who wore blue burkas. The villages seemed like another world, though. Women didn't even seem like second-class citizens, but more like third-class citizens. Cultural sensitivity was a big part of our training, and I like to think I do a better job at it than most, but we wouldn't be OK with our mothers, sisters, wives, or girlfriends being treated like those female villagers.

As I tried to shake the shock of the village elders' refusal of medical assistance for the women, I mingled a bit with the villagers. Part of my concern on these visits was always the security of the villages. Did they live under threat from the Taliban? Were criminals robbing or kidnapping villagers? Were there ethnic conflicts going on with neighboring tribes?

My interpreter and I would talk to the villagers to ascertain their security, and learn more about who lived there. As we made the rounds, a little boy approached us. He couldn't have been more than eight years old, and clearly was not well fed. The boy had a distressed expression on his face. I asked my interpreter to inquire what was wrong.

"He says he's upset because he doesn't have a job. He wants to know if you can help him find a job?"

A job?! Kid, you should be in school, I thought to myself. I was trying to ensure kids like him grew up in safety and security, but I couldn't provide economic opportunities. At the end of the day, Afghanistan is still one of poorest nations in the world. There's not much soldiers can do about that.

Obviously, having a small child ask you for a job in quiet desperation is just sad. He was so clearly devoid of the joy of childhood we all hope our children will have.

This was disturbing for an additional reason. It is true that there is often geopolitical risk in places with high populations of unemployed military age males. This kid wasn't there yet, but if the older men in his family—his father, uncles, brothers, and cousins—were adequately employed, he probably wouldn't be looking for a job. He'd be in school.

Just as they say idle hands are the Devil's playthings, large groups of unemployed men who have little hope or prospects makes a fertile recruitment pool for extremist organizations, like the Taliban and Al-Qaida. You don't see too many suicide bombers with a good job and a happy family at home.

10 FARAH

While I felt like we were doing good things in my intel shop, I still wanted to get out to an ETT. That's the mission I had trained for. It was also more in line with the professional goals that I had before I decided to leave active duty.

I asked Col. Bessler a few times if I could go to a team, but I was told I was needed at headquarters. Apparently, there was a shortage of intelligence officers going around. That explains why I was recalled in the first place. Then, after months of requesting to go to a team, I was told if I could find a replacement for myself as the ARSIC S-2 I could go. It seemed like a tall order, considering the shortage of school-trained intel guys, but it was a starting point.

I needed to find a quality officer to replace me. While I was eager to get out to a team, I wanted to make sure my guys were taken care of. Fortunately, Captain Cowen, from one of the Police Mentor Teams (PMTs), had an interest in taking my place. After his Afghanistan tour, he was going to transition from infantry to the Military Intelligence Corps, so it would be a great experience for him. Cowen was a good guy, and was a good fit.

Everyone concerned was happy, and Col. Bessler blessed the change. I was off to join my buddy Chris Garvin's team in Farah province, as the team intelligence officer. He had been commanding an ETT down there since we first got in the country, and was excited about having me join them.

Farah was dominated by Pashtun tribes, which are the traditional recruiting base of the Taliban, so the province could be a busy place. Naturally, I already knew that when I hitched a ride down to Bala Baluk with the PMT assigned to that district.

On May 1, 2009, Chris Garvin's ETT, Team Yukon, came to pick me up from the Bala Baluk PMT FOB.

Almost as if to put an exclamation point on my arrival, Team Yukon had to fight its way through a sizable ambush on the way to pick me up.

Around thirty Taliban ambushed the ETT's three HMMWVs that were en route to pick me up. There had been an intel alert of a possible ambush, but there was always an intel alert about a possible ambush, and the threatened attacks almost never occurred. This would prove to not be one of those false alarms.

The ambush kicked off as Garvin led the team down Highway 517 past Shewan, a village known to have a strong Taliban presence. The Taliban engaged the ETT with AK-47s, PKMs, and RPGs. I imagine the Taliban believed they had the advantage, as they had the element of surprise and they outnumbered the ETT about five to one. However, these insurgents immediately discovered they had picked the wrong three American trucks to attack.

The army teaches soldiers that if you want to survive an ambush, you have to attack through it. The ETT did just that, and then some. Each vehicle gunner let loose on the attacking Taliban forces with a volley of fire from the top-mounted M2 .50 caliber heavy machine guns, MK-19 automatic grenade launchers, and M240B medium machine guns. They laid waste to the numerically superior ambushing force, killing at least a dozen Taliban.

The HMMWVs were a bit shot up, but all the American personnel were fine, and they continued along their way to Bala Baluk to pick me up. It was just another day on Team Yukon. This seemed to foreshadow things to come.

Welcome to Farah.

11 THE BATTLE OF GARANI

On the morning of May 4, there were two quick knocks on my window. "Uku, you up?"

"Yeah man," I lied from inside my sleeping bag. I could recognize Garvin's voice anywhere.

"Come to the team room. We've got a meeting with the Kandak commander."

"All right, dude. I'll be right there." With that, Garvin left. I had no clue what the meeting was about. I climbed out of my sleeping bag, which was set on top of my plastic-wrapped mattress. As I put on my pants and laced up my boots, the only sound in the room was the blowing of the Iranian-made Chigo air conditioner (when, like that day, the generators were actually working). I was sure that the Soviet soldiers who occupied this room over twenty years ago would have appreciated having one of those.

The weather report online said that Farah city had been in the mid to high 100s Fahrenheit. In reality, it'd been in the high 110s to the low 120s, and was getting hotter. Today looked like it was going to be another scorcher.

I always told my guys in Herat, "Be ready every time you leave the FOB. No one is going to tell you when you wake up, 'Today is the day you're going to get into a gun fight.'" The wake-up call I had just gotten from Garvin was about as close as the warning gets.

It wasn't a meeting with just the Kandak commander. The provincial police chief and the provincial intelligence chief were there, as well as the commander of one of the US Marine Corps units. The Taliban were massing in the village of Shewan, preparing to attack the Shewan ANA garrison. "You embarrassed them on May first," said Lt. Col. Namatullah, through a translator.

The Taliban's May 1 attempt to ambush the ETT sent to pick me up just three days early had gone badly for them. Instead of running away, like the Taliban expected, the team stood and fought. At ranges of as close as twenty-five meters, three HMMWVs had fought off a numerically superior enemy. Fighting season had begun in Farah province.

The Kandak and the police would bring extra personnel and supplies to reinforce the Shewan garrison and the police checkpoints in the area. The ETT would accompany the Kandak, and the PMT would accompany the police. The marines would not be going out with us, but would to ready to roll out if we needed help. After the Afghan leaders left the room, the marine commander gave us a reassurance we would repeatedly receive, "We will always be there to QRF [quick reaction force] American forces."

Thirty minutes later, we were rolling out the gate, ready for a fight. I commanded Yukon 2, the last of the three trucks in the ETT element. Captain Henry manned the dual-mounted MK-19 automatic grenade launcher and M240B machine gun. Sergeant First Class Smith drove, and Staff Sergeant "Doc" Healy, our medic, was in the backseat, along with an interpreter. With a full crew and a trunk loaded down with lots of ammunition, we headed down Highway 517 toward Shewan, one of the biggest Taliban hotbeds in western Afghanistan.

After an hour of relatively peaceful driving, we approached the Ganjabad police checkpoint. My vehicle, along with Yukon 7, Master Sergeant Sammons's vehicle, pulled forward while Captain Garvin coordinated planning. It was immediately noticeable that people were leaving the area.

A white Toyota station wagon pulled up to Yukon 7's position. The car was stopped, and the people in it were questioned. Staff Sergeant Melson came up on the radio, "Yukon 6, this is Yukon 47. We talked to this guy leaving with his family. He says the Taliban showed up at his house, and told him and his family to leave. Over." For the next hour and a half, we watched civilians fleeing the area. One guy piled his entire family on a farm tractor just to get them out. Everyone said the same thing, "The Taliban took over our homes and told us to leave."

As the planning process with the Afghan security forces was nearing an end, we started to hear machine gun fire to the northeast of our position. Police in that area appeared to be engaged with the Taliban. There was sporadic gunfire along with an occasional explosion, but nothing was coming at my vehicle or Yukon 7.

Planning came to an end, and Yukon 6, Captain Garvin's truck, came to link up with Yukon 7 and us. It was time to push out. Tan-colored Ford Rangers, mounted with machine guns and filled with solders from the Kandak, came up with Garvin. At 1330 hours, it was time to head toward Shewan and the Taliban.

Just as we started to pull out, I heard Henry in my headset, "Three ANP Rangers just pulled out down Ganjabad Road." Ganjabad Road forked off of Highway 517 to the left. It was a dirt road that headed toward the explosions we'd heard earlier. "They look like they're by themselves," noted Henry. The PMT didn't know anything about their movement.

"Yukon 6, this is Denali 3. We're going to turn around and accompany them." One of the PMT Cougars started to turn around.

As I looked out the left side of Yukon 2 at the three police Rangers, I commented dryly, "That looks like a terrible idea." Boom! The words were barely out of my mouth when the three police Rangers came under heavy volumes of enemy fire. The trucks were stopped, and the police were simply trying to get out of this open field alive.

Denali 3 was headed toward the police, but they were the only ones. Garvin quickly made a decision, and changed our mission, "All Yukon elements, this is Yukon 6. Let's turn 'er around and go help 'em."

"Yukon 7, roger."

"Yukon 2, roger that."

My truck was in the trail position as we moved slowly up Ganjabad Road. It was a terrible place to fight from. The narrow dirt road had irrigation ditches on either side, so vehicles could only move forward and backward. Henry took up a position watching the nine o'clock position, as the column began to creep down the road, directly into enemy fire.

At this point, the heavens opened up on us. All at once, we came under heavy volumes of AK-47, machine gun, rocket-propelled grenades (RPGs), and mortar fire. The Taliban was firing at us from a walled compound in the village of Ganjabad, to our one o'clock. "I don't have a shot. Yukon 6 is in the way," Henry updated us. Yukon 2 pushed forward into all this without returning fire, waiting for a clear shot.

During that initial volley, around ten RPGs were fired at our column. An RPG hit the ground in front of Yukon

6, and one of the tailfins broke off. The fin bounced through the air, right over the head of Yukon 6's gunner Sergeant Anderson, and landed ten meters in front of my truck.

"RPG!" Boom!

"G*****n!"

"F***, that was close."

Yukon 2 kept pushing forward, waiting for a clear shot. As we continued approaching the enemy, I looked out the window to the right, and saw seven police officers lying in the ditch, not moving. "Oh s**t, are they dead?" I said, mostly to myself. Just as the words came out, I saw them start to crawl back in the direction we were coming from.

As we passed the police, a mortar exploded no more than two meters from the trailing officer. That was about five meters to the two o'clock of Yukon 2. I was certain that the Afghan was dead, but as the smoke cleared, he started making his way back with his group. *Lucky b*****d*, I thought.

As Yukon 6 crept up the road, deeper into the kill zone, Sergeant Wood, the team's only mortarman, would periodically hop out and fire 60 mm mortars back at the enemy position. Yukon 6 finally cleared our line of sight as it curved around the bend in the road. Yukon 2 had yet to return fire. Garvin's truck was out of our way, but there were still dismounted police between the enemy and us.

"You want me to fire over them?"

"Yeah, go ahead and engage," I told Henry. With that, the MK-19 and M240B came alive. Yukon 2 was in the fight. As we pushed forward, all US vehicles continued to come under heavy fire. Mortars and RPGs randomly exploded around us.

Yukon 6 pulled up to the lead position, so Yukon 7 was directly in front of my vehicle. Our small element couldn't advance any further due to the volume of fire we were receiving, so after the police had been recovered, we opted to head back to Ganjabad Road to regroup. Unfortunately, Yukon 7 reversed into the irrigation ditch on the driver's side.

It was bad. Yukon 7 was stuck on its side at a forty-five-degree angle, in the mud. Staff Sergeant Boone, the driver, tried to gun the accelerator a couple of times, but they weren't going anywhere. My vehicle pulled up behind Yukon 7 to tow them out. Time was of the essence. We were in contact with the enemy, and taking a lot of fire.

As soon as we pulled into position behind Yukon 7, Doc Healy and I hopped out to hook up the tow cables. Melson jumped out of the gun turret, and managed to get there first. I moved up to the front of Yukon 7 so I could direct Boone when he reversed.

"We're good," yelled Melson.

I signaled to Boone. He gunned it in reverse. Yukon 7 sank deeper in the mud. *God, I hope we don't have to thermite this truck*, I thought. The ARSIC had destroyed a five-ton truck that was irrecoverably stuck in the desert a couple of months earlier, with thermite grenades.

At that point, a miscommunication occurred. Master Sergeant Sammons seemed to have been thinking the same thing as I was. He told Boone to get out of the truck. Smith had no intention of giving up, though. He pulled around to the front of Yukon 7 just as Boone was climbing out of the turret.

Melson hooked up the tow cables, and Yukon 2 started pulling. Only then did Melson and I realize there was no one in the driver's seat. Not only that, but the wheels were turned the wrong direction. If we didn't get

Yukon 2 to stop, the axle could be damaged, and Yukon 7 wouldn't be going anywhere.

"What the f*** are you doing out of the truck?" yelled Melson.

"Sammons told me to get out," Boone responded. It was confusion while under fire, in a bad situation.

At that moment, Sammons, with a thermite in hand, sent a text message to the ARSIC Tactical Operations Center (TOC) over the HMMWVs communications systems. "On side. Send help." We were in trouble. The TOC would call the marines.

Melson and I were yelling at Henry to tell Smith to stop pulling, but Henry was shooting at the Taliban positions, and he couldn't hear us. Just as Henry stopped firing to look back, he saw the thermite grenade that Melson threw at him to get his attention (the pin was still in it). Of all things, Henry and Melson started arguing. Emotions were high. This little comedy of errors could have been funny, if not for the fact that one well-placed Taliban mortar could kill half of Team Yukon. We really needed to get moving.

"Shut the f*** up! Let's go!" I yelled.

Melson climbed into the driver's seat through the gunner's turret. Smith and Melson gunned it at the same time, and Yukon 7 was pulled out of the ditch.

Thank God.

Yukon 7 was now in the rear position. It was dripping mud that looked like chocolate malt with random bits of hay in it. Almost everyone climbed back in the trucks. As we started backing the HMMWVs out, I noticed that Yukon 7's Afghan interpreter was squatting in a ditch on the side of the road, looking scared to death. I waved for him to get back in his truck.

The column started creeping backward away from the enemy position at the one o'clock that we'd been taking fire from. Suddenly, we started taking fire from the village of Garani, to our nine o'clock. The compounds in Garani were almost 500 meters away, on the other side of open fields.

Now we were moving really slowly. We were under fire, driving backward through the rearview mirror, and had dismounted ANA around us. I directed seven Afghan soldiers to use our vehicle as cover while they were pulling back on foot.

It's difficult to understate the look that the Afghan soldiers gave me as we were pulling back in our up-armored HMMWVs. It's probably similar to the look you would get if you abandoned your child in the woods and drove off. Their eyes screamed, "Why are you leaving me here?"

The backward movement of the column stalled. Henry kept returning fire toward enemy positions to our nine o'clock. The Afghan soldiers took cover in an irrigation ditch. I got out of Yukon 2, and using the armored hood for cover, returned fire at the enemy positions with my M4.

Col. Bessler would later verbally reprimand me for this decision, calling it an instance of cowboying. However, it seemed difficult to inspire Afghan soldiers by just staring at them from the other side of bulletproof glass. As I leaned against the hood of my vehicle, firing at Taliban positions, the Afghan soldiers stared at me like I was crazy. But having them look at me like I was a madman was better than them looking at me like I was abandoning them.

Don't look at me! Shoot at the Taliban! I thought to myself. But there was no point yelling at them. They didn't understand English, anyway.

I noticed a column of dismounted fighters in Garani moving eastbound. I tried to tell Henry, but nobody could hear me over all the fire, so I engaged the fighters myself.

When the fire subsided, the column continued backward. As Yukon 2 backed into a covered position, I walked out of the danger area with those seven Afghan soldiers, using the vehicle for cover. We all sighed a deep breath. It was 1630 hours. We'd been fighting for three hours, and the day was nowhere near over.

During a lull in the fight that lasted a couple of hours, we reorganized the Kandak to get them in the fight, and two teams of marines had arrived. With that, this mixed force took the fight to the Taliban. After hours of fighting, completely outnumbered, we finally got some close air support (CAS), which dropped seven 500-pound bombs and one 2,000-pound bomb on Taliban positions.

Next, the marines led a dismounted group of Afghan soldiers on foot to assault Taliban positions in the village.

Even after the bombing, the Taliban were putting up a fight. The ETT and PMT provided support fire, as the combined USMC/ANA force advanced upon the village across an open field. However, there was little we could do once they entered the village but listen to the gun fire and wait.

The assault was largely successful. Unfortunately, one marine and one ANA soldier were wounded, but no friendly forces were killed.

As daylight faded, we got ready for a long night. We had had a long day of fighting in an attempt to dislodge Taliban forces who were terrorizing the civilian population. Thanks to those three ANP trucks that inexplicably took off down Ganjabad Road, we gave up the initiative, and fought under very nonideal circumstances, but we managed to do some good work. Thus, we had no intention of letting Taliban forces sneak back in overnight.

The marines were able to call for a UH-60 Blackhawk helicopter to resupply us with more ammunition and take out the wounded. It came in under the cover of night to avoid presenting a target for lingering insurgents. With that, we rearmed before moving into our security positions, where we would spend the rest of the evening.

We opened up a few MREs for dinner inside our HMMWVs, but after darkness fell, it quickly became nearly pitch black. There is nearly no ambient light in rural Afghanistan. A shot hadn't been fired in hours, but we had no intention of being the victims of a counterattack overnight. We maintained 50 percent security through the night.

The idea was that half the forces would sleep for an hour, while the other half pulled security, wearing NVGs. However, it's not like that hour of rack time is particularly restful. You sit in a HMMWV with your body armor on, and try to get sixty minutes of sleep, sitting upright.

Because the HMMWV is up-armored, we could take our Kevlar helmets off with the doors shut, but we had them and our M4s within arms' reach, and we each had an M9 pistol on our person. If you tried to get some sleep in the backseats, your body armor might start to cut off circulation in your thighs due to the limited leg room.

All in all, there was little sleep to be had. I may have closed my eyes for ninety minutes or so during the course of the night. Mostly, I waited for the inevitable Taliban counterattack. It never came.

The sun rose without incident. We suffered no Taliban attacks overnight. *Thank God.* We got our orders to pull up stakes, get on the road, and get back to base.

12 THE AFTERMATH

Team Yukon returned to the FOB at 1100 hours on May 5, 2009, after nearly twenty-four hours of continuous combat operations. The firefight lasted for a total of eight hours, but all of our people were coming back alive.

"Everyone be back on the trucks at 1400," Sammons informed us.

We were exhausted, but the trucks and weapons needed to be refitted so we could roll out at a moment's notice. So we were going to get three hours of down time before getting back to work. Intelligence reports said that for those first three hours of the fight, when we were out there by ourselves, we were outnumbered by as much as ten to one.

We soon began to feel the aftermath of the prolonged gunfight. The media got involved. Around 1700 hours, with two and a half hours of sleep under my belt, I found the first news articles that began to trickle out about our "fierce ground battle," as the Associated Press called it in one article. The articles mentioned civilian casualties from the air strikes.

Many people don't realize that the Taliban is very savvy when it comes to using the free press against us. From the perspective of a soldier on the ground, there are two things wrong with how most western media operate in Afghanistan.

First, in the effort to be first to press, reporters seem willing to quote anyone who claims to have information. They don't seem to check the background of the people giving them that information before quoting them in international media. The problem is that most Taliban supporters won't tell you they are Taliban supporters.

Second, most news articles written about western Afghanistan were written by people who have never been to western Afghanistan. Over 4,000 articles were published in the aftermath of the Garani bombings. I'm unaware of any of those journalists setting foot in Garani.

It would have been possible. We went back to Garani three more times to escort various investigations.

There were examples of these problems after Garani. First, former Bala Baluk district sub-governor Mohammad Nieem Qadderdan was widely quoted in international media regarding the "atrocities" of the American bombing. The problem is that Mr. Qadderdan was the *former* sub-governor *because* he was Taliban. Not the most credible source.

Second, quoting the Afghan villagers on numbers of civilian casualties is notoriously unreliable. People who have spent time in rural Afghanistan will be familiar with math-related issues, such as being told of "a hundred Taliban traveling in four Toyota Corollas." It is also problematic asking villagers how many family members they lost, because the government pays them per family member. There is a financial incentive for poor villagers to inflate those numbers. Direct evidence of that was seen after Garani, as initial claims stated that 120–130 civilians were killed.

In the end, the US government and the Afghan government disagreed on the number of civilians killed. The American investigation showed around twenty-six civilians killed. The Afghan investigation said over a hundred were killed. Odd, since both parties toured the battlefield together. It was especially frustrating when we heard stories of Taliban fragging families in their homes (which they had taken over to fight from), so they could blame it on American forces. The Taliban refused to let some villagers leave their homes while the Taliban fought from their confines. Those unfortunate individuals were killed because it was the Taliban's intent. Even a single civilian casualty is a bad thing, but this had been a bad day.

The guys on the ground went from feeling the pride of taking on a numerically superior force and winning, to feeling like the media thought they were a bunch of baby killers.

Our intelligence told us that over sixty-five Taliban were killed, but sadly, innocent people felt the pain of war, too. We could have left Garani after we'd pulled out of the kill zone, but what would we have taught the Afghan National Security Forces? Show up, get your butt kicked, then go home? Garani was a tactical victory, but it became a media defeat.

EPILOGUE

It has taken five years for this project to see the light of day. Garani was the first time I saw combat, but it wasn't the last. I once had an RPG fly right by my HMMMV. I'm not even sure how many times I've been shot at, but I do recall the round that hit my HMMMV door. Thankfully it was up-armored. Twice (that I know of) we narrowly missed hitting IEDs on the road. Like Staff Sergeant Anderson said, "Combat ain't cool. It's exciting, but it ain't cool." Through all of this, we were fortunate enough to not lose any Americans on my ETT in Farah, but that is not to say we didn't see friendly casualties.

Five years offers a lot of time to gain distance and perspective on an experience like deployment to

Afghanistan. I wrote this book within the first forty-five days of my redeployment to the United States. Emotions were still very high. In the course of a couple of weeks, I moved from the backwaters of Afghanistan to New York City. To say it was an adjustment would be an epic understatement. I tried to get my thoughts and emotions onto the page as quickly as I could, while they were still fresh in me. Then, after a lengthy delay in this project, I considered adding to my previous text to help complete the story for the reader. However, I decided against it, so as not to dilute the tale.

My experience was not particularly remarkable. That is to say, there are a lot of military men and women who have tales just like mine. However, all of our experiences were remarkable. The United States fought the longest war in its history in Afghanistan. For many of those years, we simultaneously fought a conflict in Iraq that was longer and more vicious than I believe most anyone thought it would be. All the while, most Americans were able to go on about their lives, as we called upon a relatively small number of our people to bear the burden of those years of war. I've known people who literally spent three, four, or five years of their lives in those war zones.

In the years since I've returned and taken off the uniform, my countrymen have been very kind. Whether or not they supported the wars, they say, "Thank you for your service." The Vietnam veterans seem very happy that the Afghanistan and Iraq veterans have been treated better than they were. The people I've known respect that we fought so they didn't have to. They don't know what it's like to go to work and think, *I might not survive today*, but I hope this brief memoir will help provide a view of what life was like for us.

While in Afghanistan, I read Tolstoy's *War and Peace*. It was interesting to be at war and read about Napoleon's invasion of Imperial Russia, a war that took place almost 200 years earlier. The more things change, the more they stay the same. One very true constant I noticed is that when you go away to war, people don't hit pause on their lives, waiting for you to get back. Your friends and loved ones will have a lot of experiences without you while you're gone: birthdays, anniversaries, weddings, deaths, or just the everyday experiences that you don't appreciate until you're not present for them. (Personally, I spent my thirtieth birthday alone in a tent in Kabul.)

Your friends and loved ones will probably change somewhat. You most certainly will change. As much as you wish it, things will not be exactly the same when you get back as when you left.

In addition, I think every veteran I know has at least a mild case of post-traumatic stress disorder (PTSD). We don't like to talk about it, and we certainly don't like to admit it, but it seems like everyone has a hard time when they get back, in one way or another.

It can take its toll on you, the knowledge that there are people out there who would love to see you dead. Every time you set foot outside the wire, there is a chance they will take a shot. Even inside the wire, there is a chance that a mortar attack, an insurgent pretending to be a friendly, or a full-on assault could kill you. Of course, the threat of attack pales in comparison to actually being attacked. Trust me, getting shot at is a highly overrated experience. I generally recommend against it. Personally, I've had more than a couple of bad dreams since I redeployed.

Five years removed from the experience, I'm proud of my service for my country. Given the opportunity, I'd do it all over again. The experience has cost me in some ways, but it has helped make me the man I am today. I had the privilege of serving alongside some of the finest Americans I have ever known. I hope our countrymen continue to give these warriors the credit they deserve. To all my brothers- and sisters-in-arms out there...thank you for your service.

Oritse Justin Uku

August 13, 2014

PHOTOS

S-2 shop: Captain Uku, Sergeant Lloyd, Senior Airman Sweatman, and Petty Officer Swanberg (left to right)

Afghan village homes in Bala Baluk district, Farah province

A predawn, joint Afghan-US-Italian combat patrol

ETT HMMWV pulling security with M2 and M240B machine guns

Joint Afghan-US-Italian combat patrol

ETT HMMWV pulling security with MK19; Italian army armored vehicle in the distance

ANA soldiers in Ford Ranger with PKM machine gun

Captain Uku with recent HMMWV combat damage

Captains Uku, Garvin and Henry (left to right)

Sergeant Anderson resting during a break in fighting with the Taliban

Captain Uku during break in fighting, Italian army vehicles in the background

Captains Henry (left) and Garvin (right), with Spanish embedded reporters

UH-60 Blackhawk MEDEVAC helicopter arriving to evacuate ANA casualties

Captain Uku in Dress Blue Uniform

GLOSSARY

ANA—Afghan National Army.

ANP—Afghan National Police.

ANSF—Afghan National Security Forces, including the ANA, the ANP, and the Afghan Border Patrol.

ARSIC—Afghan Regional Security Integration Command.

CAS—Close Air Support is air action by fixed-wing and rotary-wing aircraft against hostile targets that are in close proximity to friendly forces, and requires detailed integration of each air mission with the fire and movement of those forces. (Joint Publication 3-09.3, 2009).

IED—Improvised Explosive Device. A device placed or fabricated in an improvised manner, incorporating destructive, lethal, noxious, pyrotechnic, or incendiary chemicals, and designed to destroy, incapacitate, harass, or distract. It may incorporate military stores, but is normally devised from nonmilitary components. (DoD Directive 2000.19E, 2006).

ETT—Embedded Training Team.

FOB—Forward Operating Base.

HMMWV—High Mobility Multipurpose Wheeled Vehicle, commonly known as the Humvee.

IRR—Individual Ready Reserve.

ISAF—International Security Assistance Force.

Kandak—A battalion in the Afghan National Army.

M2—A .50 caliber, heavy machine gun.

M240B—A 7.62 mm belt-fed, gas-operated medium machine gun.

M4—A shorter and lighter variant of the 5.56 mm M16A2 assault rifle.

M9—The Beretta 9 mm semiautomatic pistol.

MEDEVAC—Medical Evacuation.

MITT—Military Transition Team

MK19—An American 40 mm belt-fed automatic grenade launcher, commonly known as the Mark-19.

MRE—Meal, Ready-to-Eat is a self-contained, individual field ration in lightweight packaging, bought by the US military for its service members for use in combat or other field conditions.

NCO—Noncommissioned Officer.

Nom de Guerre—An assumed name under which a person engages in combat or some other activity or enterprise.

NVG—Night Vision Goggles.

PKM—A 7.62 mm general-purpose machine gun designed in the Soviet Union and currently in production in Russia.

PMT—Police Mentor Team.

PTSD—Post-Traumatic Stress Syndrome.

QRF—Quick Reaction Force is a combat arms unit that is capable of rapid response to developing situations.

RPG—Rocket-Propelled Grenade.

SVBIED—A Suicide Vehicle-Borne Improvised Explosive Device.

Thermite grenade—Typically used in both an anti-materiel role and in the partial destruction of equipment; the latter being common when time is not available for safer or more thorough methods.

TOC—Tactical Operations Center.

ABOUT THE AUTHOR

Oritse (pronounced Or-ree-sha) Justin Uku, having spent six and a half years in uniform, embodies the qualities of an officer and a gentleman. His travels cover a wide spectrum of interest from the beaches of Rio de Janeiro to the palaces of Vienna, from the Great Wall of China to the Great Barrier Reef.

As a US Army captain in military intelligence, he served overseas in South Korea, Germany, and Afghanistan. Oritse's military decorations include a Bronze Star Medal and a Combat Action Badge for exemplary service in direct fire combat.

Oritse has a Bachelor of Arts (BA) in History and a Master of Business Administration (MBA) from Boston College. After his Operation Enduring Freedom (OEF) deployment, he also earned a Master of International Affairs (MIA) from Columbia University. He studied abroad at the University of Melbourne in Australia.

Oritse speaks conversational German, elementary Spanish, and limited Japanese. He currently resides in Chicago, Illinois in the United States.

Made in the USA
Lexington, KY
10 December 2014